A BOOK IS A PRESENT YOU CAN OPEN AGAIN AND AGAIN

This Book Belongs To

Nancy Love.

from Robert
Christmas 1989.

IN·A·CANADIAN GARDEN

Nicole Eaton & Hilary Weston

PHOTOGRAPHY by FREEMAN PATTERSON

VIKING
STUDIO
BOOKS

VIKING STUDIO BOOKS
Published by the Penguin Group
Penguin Books Canada Ltd., 2801 John Street,
Markham, Ontario, Canada L3R 1B4
Penguin Books Ltd., 27 Wrights Lane,
London W8 5TZ, England
Viking Penguin Inc., 40 West 23rd Street,
New York, New York 10010, USA
Penguin Books Australia Ltd, Ringwood,
Victoria, Australia
Penguin Books (NZ) Ltd, 182–190 Wairau
Road, Auckland 10, New Zealand

Penguin Books Ltd, Registered Offices:
Harmondsworth, Middlesex, England

First published 1989

10 9 8 7 6 5 4 3 2 1

Printed and bound in Italy

Canadian Cataloguing in Publication Data

Eaton, Nicole
  In a Canadian garden

ISBN 0-670-82166-7

1. Photography of gardens – Canada. 2. Gardens –
Canada – Pictorial works. I. Weston, Hilary.
II. Patterson, Freeman 1937– III. Title.

TR662.E28 1989   779′.97126′0971   C87-094897-0

British Library Cataloguing in Publication Data
Available
American Library of Congress Cataloguing in
Publication Data Available

Contents

Acknowledgements

We are most grateful to Humber Nursery Ltd., Yoder Canada Ltd. and Bruce Jensen Nurseries Inc. for underwriting some of Freeman Patterson's travelling expenses. Their generosity will benefit the Canadian Environmental Educational Foundation towards which all our royalties from this book will be directed.

In a Canadian Garden was made possible because many people all across Canada helped us. Some researched and suggested gardens for us to see, some offered much appreciated hospitality, some drove us around for long hours and some did all of the above.

To Harvey Lowe and Ann Nations, Joan Patterson, Martha Evans, Joan Courtois, Jacques Courtois Jr, Francis Cabot, Shirley Robertson, Alex Wilson, Betty Nelson, Patricia DeGroote, A.G. Searle, Rob Serbin, Brenda Norris, Susan Perrin, Judy Burgess, Wendy Rebanks, Georgine Coutu, Helen Birks, Donald Miller, Kelly Meighen, Brenda McCarthy, Betty How, Jane Crosbie, Jeannie Southam, Frank Kershaw, Tannis Richardson, Terri Clarke, P.N.D. Seymour, Meme Battle, David Matthews, Norm Franklin, Dorothy Dawson, J.R. Begg, Wayne Kennedy, M.K. Chamandy, Brian Bixley, Russ Kehler, Robin Matthysen, we offer our deepest gratitude.

We would also like to express our appreciation to Freeman Patterson for putting both his heart and huge talent into this project. To Kay Schmidt we say thank you for retyping all the texts at least once. We are indebted to David Kilgour, our editor, who offered both his experience and support and made putting this book together a pleasure.

Nicole Eaton
Hilary Weston

I want to express my respect for Nicole Eaton and Hilary Weston for the quality of their research into private Canadian gardens, and my appreciation to the gardeners for their unfailing hospitality and kindness. Thank you all. It has been a wonderful experience.

Freeman Patterson

Editors' Preface

When we set out two years ago to find the gardens portrayed in this book, our goal was relatively modest: we wanted to prove to ourselves and to other interested gardeners that a Canadian garden is not a contradiction in terms. We knew the task would not be an easy one, but we were not prepared for the sheer wealth and diversity we found.

Voltaire once dismissed Canada as *"quelques arpents de neige."* How wrong he was! We inhabit a vast country that encompasses dozens of climatic and geographical zones and harbours countless plant species, indigenous, introduced and hybridized. And the different gardening traditions immigrants have brought with them from around the world have added whole new dimensions to the landscape.

In a Canadian Garden is an appreciation, a celebration of just some of the most beautiful gardens we have seen. It is not a how-to guide to gardening in Canada, nor is it a comprehensive survey of all the "best" gardens in the country—no one book could accomplish that.

In our quest we crossed Canada several times and saw hundreds of gardens. Because we were interested only in private gardens, we had to depend on the kindness and generosity of people who gave us their time, opened up their gardens and homes to us and suggested other places we might see. We are most grateful for their help.

Our final choice is avowedly idiosyncratic. Like most of the people we met across the country, we are avid amateur gardeners rather than horticultural experts or formally trained landscape architects. We looked, above all, for gardens with a distinctive, coherent aesthetic, whether they reflected our personal taste or not, those that were the result of one or two people's particular vision. Our other criteria included horticultural interest, variety and, where possible, regional representation. But when a difficult choice had to be made, aesthetics and charm won the day.

We started out with preconceived ideas. Were all the great gardens on the west coast? Not at all: Mary Talbot's soft, painterly garden in northern Alberta is just one of the surprises we discovered in a harsh climatic zone. In Ontario and Québec, bastions of tradition, we looked for great herbaceous gardens and found instead Amy Stewart's rock-terraced hillside garden in Caledon and Al Cummings's tiny, architectural gem in Toronto. On the east coast we expected to find austere, rocky gardens that matched the inhospitable but magnificent elements of the seaside. Instead, we saw Walter Ostrom's rare botanical specimens and Marguerite Vaughan's colourful manorial garden in St Andrews. In Québec we visited the spectacular garden of Frank Cabot—twenty-eight gardens in one—perhaps the best-known garden in the country. Searching for a Japanese garden in British Columbia, we found the romance and exuberance of Shirley Beach's rose garden and the wisteria and dappled greens of Elaine Corbet's alpinish jewel. In the western interior we expected prairie fields full of native flowers, but were captivated by the grassy lanes and spare plantings of Mary Dover's garden near Calgary.

Mary Dover's garden deserves particular mention here because, to more traditional gardeners, it may not seem at first glance to be a garden at all. Mary cherishes the wilderness of the landscape in which she lives, and she has chosen to "edit" it rather than tame it. With the exception of one extravagant planting of peonies, she has added only small traces of herself—a fruit tree here, a clump of flowers there—to the land. But for all its ruggedness, Mary's garden is every bit as planned and deliberate as a more formal one such as Harvey Sobel's in Hamilton.

Gardening in Canada is still in its infancy. The gardeners featured in this book often work in relative isolation, with only a few books or interested neighbours to inspire them. Most of them do all their own digging, planting, weeding, fertilizing and designing. And although clubs and horticultural societies play an increasing role in bringing Canadian gardeners together, we still can't boast the highly organized networks in, say, Britain or France. Perhaps this will change as interest grows.

Our own gardens are included here at our publisher's insistence. They felt that we could not ask others to share their gardens if we were not prepared to do the same.

Just as each garden presented here is a personal statement, the accompanying text is an expression of the gardener's particular satisfactions and frustrations. The writing is as varied as the gardens themselves and ranges from the lyrical to the technical. Some gardeners treasure the history of their land, others botanical specimens they have lovingly cultivated; a surprising number of people write eloquently about the joy of their gardens in winter.

To photograph the gardens, we hoped to find someone who would not merely document them but who would also bring to the work a unifying personal vision.

We were delighted when Freeman Patterson agreed to work with us. His photographs were often a revelation not only to us but even to the gardeners themselves, acting as complements rather than adjuncts to the texts.

For all the gardens we saw, we know there are thousands more we didn't see. This, then, is just a beginning, a small recognition of the genius and individuality of Canadian gardeners. We have found the whole experience inspiring, enriching—and a lot of fun. We hope the results will encourage readers to pursue their own gardening visions.

Nicole Eaton & Hilary Weston
Toronto
January 1989

Photographer's Preface

One overcast November day, after the first snow had transformed my cedar trail, I made the first photograph for *In a Canadian Garden*. Between that image and the last, a September picture of the Stewarts' garden near Caledon, Ontario, I hopscotched back and forth across Canada five times. For most of the spring, my pace was leisurely, but because weather conditions delayed the peak of the flower season in some regions and advanced it in others, gardeners all over the country started phoning me in the second half of June. One memorable July day I photographed in Barbara Frum's Don Mills garden in the morning and in two Vancouver gardens in the late afternoon and evening. It was an unusual shooting schedule for somebody accustomed to photographing wilderness and other natural areas at his own pace, and there were moments when I longed for the slower rhythms of wild places.

A garden, by definition, is not wild. No matter how much it follows the natural contours of the land or how many local native plants it contains, a garden exists only because of a gardener. Therefore, gardens tend to be as different from one another as the people who create them.

The editors recognized that many Canadian gardeners respond to the natural aesthetics of their particular environment, and they selected several gardens for this book that are wild or partly wild. Both Jocelyne Turcotte's garden in Québec and Walter Ostrom's in Nova Scotia begin with domestic plantings near the house that gradually give way to seasonal displays of wild flowers. Much of Princess Abkhazi's Victoria garden seems to flow, as she says, like a river—the pools and plantings of low shrubs, grasses and perennials accentuating and intensifying descending sweeps of long rock ledges. The rest of her garden is a small, spectacularly beautiful rhododendron forest. When I die, I want to go to Princess Abkhazi's forest. Harvey Sobel's small city garden in Hamilton, Ontario is patterned after a great French tradition of garden design, yet has clearly personal features that tie it to his house and its interior decoration. Such is the diversity of Canadian gardens—and Canadian gardeners.

Although I have been a lifelong gardener myself, I nevertheless began this project thinking of a garden more as an ornament than as a dynamic work of art. Long before I completed it, I realized how wrong I was. A garden grows and changes as its maker changes. Rippled by the creative winds of our imagination and disturbed frequently by our dreams, a garden seldom provides us with a clear mirror image of ourselves, yet is forever tantalizing us with imperfect but revealing glimpses of something else. When we work to create a fine garden, we are using the natural materials of Earth—sunlight, water, soil and plants—to create an expression of our better selves. Every gardener, like every garden, is a work in progress.

There is a natural connection between gardening and photography. Both are highly visual pursuits, and success in both depends on developing an appreciation of good visual design or composition.

The pictures in this book were made with photographic equipment available to and easily used by any gardener. For my Minolta 35mm cameras, I selected three Minolta lenses: a 28–85mm zoom lens for overall views and small sections of gardens, a 70–210mm zoom lens to make difficult or distant spots more visually accessible and to compress distance and a 100mm macro lens for occasional close-ups of individual blossoms. Occasionally I attached a polarizing filter to the lenses in order to eliminate unwanted reflections in water or glare on leaves, or to enrich the blue of the sky and to define the shape of clouds more clearly. Because colour films seldom reproduce the shades of natural blue pigments accurately, I used a pale blue 82A filter for blue and purple flowers.

Almost without exception, I placed my cameras on a sturdy but compact and lightweight Manfrotto ART–190 tripod, which I fitted with a Leitz ball-and-socket head. The tripod not only enabled me to make photographs in low light, but also made it possible for me to examine each composition carefully and to make adjustments easily. Also, by using the tripod, I could compose a picture in advance of a desired lighting effect and be ready to press the shutter release the moment it occurred.

At the beginning of the project I made identical photographs on different films and quickly chose Fujichrome 50 and 100 films for their outstanding ability to register greens of every nuance and (along with the 82A filter) to render the difficult blue flowers with accuracy and brilliance, while providing excellent fidelity and saturation of all other hues. I particularly noted that these two films have the capacity to absorb annoying minor glare from glossy leaves and other reflecting surfaces, making the use of my polarizing filter unnecessary in many situations.

While I always hoped for overcast or rainy conditions

when I visited a garden, because soft indirect light reduces harsh contrasts and seems to make colours glow, I had my fair share of sunshine. When clear skies and bright sunlight were likely to be a problem during the day, I usually began photographing in the early evening and continued until half an hour after sunset. Often I was shooting again before sunrise. These are also times when many people most enjoy their gardens. Because nights were short during the peak period of my project, more than one gardener found me curled up asleep under a bush during the late morning or early afternoon.

Freeman Patterson
Shampers Bluff
January 1989

A bench in Mary Dover's garden,
Midnapore, Alberta.

IN·A·CANADIAN
GARDEN

THE GARDEN OF

ARTHUR ERICKSON
VANCOUVER, BRITISH COLUMBIA

Above left: *A combination of grasses, leaves and rock gives this garden a naturalistic, cool effect.*

Above right: *A planting of yellow Lysimachia nummularia softens the hard edge of the pond.*

Right: *Careful planting extends the illusion of space in this small city garden.*

Far right: *A pond festooned with water-lilies is the main feature of the garden.*

I bought my home in 1958 for the charm of its English perennial border garden, a rose arbour and raspberry patch at the back, a double-lot size and southern exposure.

The robust grasses in the garden persuaded me that a low-maintenance garden would have to be based on them. I also wanted to conceal the front door of the house across the street, so a bulldozer built up a pile towards the end of the lot and continued excavating in front of it until a sufficient elevation had been reached to block out the offending door. The excavation was then lined and filled with water.

Along one flank of the hill I planted several kinds of local grasses and by the pond, spiny clump grasses from a nearby bog. Delicate grass planted in front of the pool secluded a more intimate area near the house. The rest of the hill was covered in crushed blue limestone to deter weeds

Right: *Local grasses mark the intimate area near the house.*

Far right: *The bamboo grove adds an Oriental touch.*

and promote moss between a few junipers.

The planting henceforth would reflect the Japanese technique – which I did not know at the time – of extending the perception of distance. A series of succeeding planes of planting each partially concealed the immediate plane behind it. Somehow, what is intimated, yet out of full view, suggests to the eye a greater remoteness.

One "room" of this compartmentalization of the yard is that of the pool, with its play of soft against hard edges that seem to disappear beyond the rhododendrons. Over the years I have chosen plant materials for leaf colour and texture, not blossom, so that it is essentially green.

The hill forms another room. On either side and behind grow varieties of bamboos – all grasses themselves. The plane beyond the hill is a bamboo grove shaded by existing Douglas fir and dogwood trees. A cedar hedge and Lombardy poplars barricade the outer edge of the property. The view of the poplars from the house conceals their bases and confuses the eye as to how far away they are.

I haven't tried to force the garden, apart from trimming in fall and spring. For several years poppies appeared on the hill, then disappeared. Now harebells are taking over. The pool has never been touched. Years of leafmould, rushes and wild iris cake the bottom and provide refuge for the carp. Someday it may sustain the miniature lotus covered in clear algae that is a delicacy in Japan. But, I am told, it could take about three hundred years.

THE GARDEN OF

VERONICA MILNER
QUALICUM BEACH, BRITISH COLUMBIA

The "Long-Distance Gardens" were started in 1954 after I was married; before then my husband had used the place only as a retreat from his business interests. We gave the property this name because it was so far away from my old home, and because the telephone was always ringing for my husband!

The drive to the house through the woods was a thick tangle of huckleberry and salal, and the forest was so dark that no birds chose to live there. Although I wanted the garden to retain some of its wildness, I also wanted to make it a welcome habitat for wildlife, particularly birds. We had to open up glades to let in the

Top and left: This garden was created in a forest of ancient Douglas firs on the Straits of Georgia.

Above: A pool in a glade provides a haven for birds.

light and drain excess water into pools for the birds to drink in.

We also opened up the views over the Straits of Georgia, which look like a beautiful land-locked sea, bounded by the coastal range, the mainland, the islands and the Forbidden Plateau on this island itself. But we left thousand-year-old Douglas firs and cedars that grow majestically down to the sea's edge. They are home for the kingfishers living in the banks, the eagles and the herons who use their high protection for their nests and as a lookout on their fishing grounds.

We lined these glades with a collection of specie and other rhododendrons and carpeted them with cyclamen, trillium, grey erythroniums and indigenous wild flowers.

Left: *A mature rhododendron soars above a carpet of native wild flowers.*

Above: *Thriving in the benevolent micro-climate, rhododendrons have become one of the most prominent features of this garden.*

Our house stands on a bluff high above the Straits where only 120 years ago the Indians held clambakes. Purple finches and wrens have their nests in the camellias around the house, and the humming-birds join them in the spring when the red currant comes into bloom. Here we have plantings of many small trees and shrubs such as Japanese maples, eucryphias, figs, Davidia, magnolias and cercidiphyllums, which thrive on the gentle slopes because there are no frost pockets and because they are protected by Mount Arrowsmith from all storms.

There are several regions left in British Columbia where havens such as ours can be found and nurtured. I hope that others will create a similar mixture of garden and wilderness, surrounded by the ancient trees that grow here.

Above: *The arboreal forest has been thinned to offer welcoming light and space to birds.*

Opposite: *Thousand-year-old Douglas firs and other native trees shelter the collection of rhododendrons.*

THE GARDEN OF

ANGELA BOWERING
VANCOUVER, BRITISH COLUMBIA

Gardens began for me before I knew I was a sentient being. I spent my infancy and early childhood in my grandmother's garden on Quadra Island – then a small isolated island between Vancouver Island and the mainland.

All gardens, I suspect, are founded, whether consciously or not, in the hopefulness of the dream of regaining paradise. So my childhood *imago mundi* was a garden. I remember my grandfather haying in foggy moonlit fields at dusk; I remember my grandmother's bent back and bonneted head as she stooped, weeding, mulching and picking strawberries; I remember my sister Joan and I picking apples and pears, picking gooseberries, lingonberries, raspberries and quince. All of these things are images of perfect happiness for me. The world they came from is alive now only in my memory and in my garden's remembrance of my grandmother's garden.

My mother, too, had a garden in every place we ever lived. She sifted every square inch of topsoil in her last garden by hand, so when she left it and the developers ploughed it under and paved it over, I knew I had to translate the many years I had spent reading, dreaming, remembering, imagining and planning into my own garden.

And so this garden was born.

I have an espaliered apple and an espaliered pear for the loss and recovery of paradise, two fig trees and a cherry tree, a grape arbour and a strawberry jar, a fish pond with water-lilies, and a rampant *passiflora* vine. I am deeply aware of the symbology of all these things. Gardens are remembrance and hope; they bind generations together; they promise something. The nicest thing anyone ever said to me about mine was half remonstrance: "You can't make paradise, Angela." My response was, "No, but you can try to make an *earthly* paradise."

My garden does not look like my grandmother's garden, or like my mother's gardens. It is much too self-conscious, but for all that, it owes itself to them, since it was their gardens that first engraved themselves in my heart as places of wonder and abundance.

Above: *A reflective pool in a corner of the front garden.*

Far left: *Arching sprays of* Clematis montana *climb the walls of a small trellised arbour.*

Middle left: *A striking composition of climbing pyracantha, white tulips and a bronze-leafed tree peony.*

Near left: *A rhododendron stands at the end of a pergola hung with Clematis henrii.*

*Below: A long border full of
rhododendrons and azaleas in
bloom leads to the steps running
down to the lower garden.*

THE GARDEN OF

JOSEPH SEGAL
VANCOUVER, BRITISH COLUMBIA

I have been interested in gardening since I was a kid in Edmonton and my father terraced the hill we lived on and created a garden. Wherever I have lived, we have always had a nice garden. When we moved to this property fifteen years ago, I hired Raoul Robillard, a landscape architect well known in this area, whose family had been involved with the design of the Butchart Gardens in Victoria. He suggested that we return the garden to its natural topography, which meant uncovering a ravine around the house and moving a thousand cubic yards of dirt. He then laid out the garden in a series of curving, undulating rooms. The upper part of the garden connects with the newly uncovered lower level by a grand set of tiled steps with planters set into each of the steps.

In the summer these planters are filled with alyssum, geraniums, impatiens and fibrous begonias. The bones of the various rooms are hedges and bushes that act as a foil for the massive plantings of bulbs and annuals.

In the summer the first thing I do when I get home at night is take off my tie and jacket and go out and watch the vegetables grow. In the winter, in the conservatory, I look after the

*Above left: A hanging pot of
fuchsia adds colour to a tranquil
corner of the house.*

Above right: The front gate.

*Over, left: A mature clipped
hedge in the upper garden.*

*Over, right: Pots of annuals
hanging from a cedar hedge
create a surreal effect.*

orchids because that's easy; here we also grow lemon, grapefruit and lime trees which all bear fruit, varieties of Birds of Paradise and eighteen or more huge fuchsia trees. The fuchsia trees summer out on the lower-level patio.

I wanted a spectacular garden, and it is perhaps here that Robillard's connection to the Butchart is felt, as colour is a most important component. We plant six thousand bulbs every year, as well as thousands of summer and fall bedding plants that create successive waves of colour after the spring show of azaleas, rhododendrons, camellias and magnolias.

We like to share our garden, and we open the house to a number of charities for benefits. Each year, as many as ten to twelve wedding parties—strangers to us—are photographed in the garden. Recently a photographer asked the bride to keep stepping backwards, as he wanted our waterfall in the background. She took one step too many and fell into the pool.

This garden is really a work of art, and it gives me great pleasure and pride to maintain such a sanctuary so close to the city's core.

Left: *Massive annual plantings fill all the beds of the lower garden in summer.*

Above: *In spring tulips dance down an opulent stairway.*

Right: Pyracantha clipped and trained against a cedar fence.

Above: Carefully clipped Cotoneaster dammeri *and a Japanese lantern lend a Pacific influence to the garden.*

THE ARDEN OF

ELAINE CORBET
VANCOUVER, BRITISH COLUMBIA

When I first saw this garden almost ten years ago, it appealed to me because of the view and sounds of the sea, and because it was made up of many differing parts. It is small – seventy-five by two hundred feet – so I can look after it, with the help of a friend twice a month.

The garden slopes steeply down to the west, levels out and drops straight over a rock-face. A large wisteria hangs over the rock-face and blooms heavily most years. Stone steps lead up from below and a pink *Camellia sasanqua* leans on the warm rocks, with *Iris Kaempferi* doing well in a bed moistened naturally by seepage. A small waterfall feeds a pond where maidenhair and sword ferns thrive. By the patio, *Cryptomeria japonica* and a *Rhus typhina laciniata* are trained to frame the view of Howe Sound and to hide a telephone pole below.

In the rock garden at the top of the slope is a selection of alpine plants placed, I hope, so as to form a harmonious whole. I have re-done the nearby perennial bed countless times hoping that the colours will be more to my liking.

Beside the house, *Iris unguicularis* bloom intermittently in winter. Both the young *Carpenteria californica* and the *Hebe* 'Alicia Amherst' have flowered once and I hope will do so again.

Protected by several Western red cedars (*Thuja plicata*), camellias and many rhododendrons grow, chosen primarily for the shapes and colours of their leaves. Hostas, bergenias and hellebores give other shapes and shades of green. Spring and summer colours are provided by bulbs, primulas, herbaceous perennials and ground covers. Clematis species such as C. *macropetala* and C. *texensis* grow through the larger old rhododendrons.

Trees such as a *Liquidambar styraciflua*, a *Cercidiphyllum japonicum* and an *Arbutus unedo* add height and interest, and a young *Stewartia pseudocamellia* promises to contribute to the overall effect. I must frequently remind myself to stand back and admire what all the plants are doing for my garden – often in spite of me.

Above: *Mosses and alpine plants cover a massive rock outcropping.*

Above: *A vignette of ferns, mosses and ground cover is typical of this carefully thought-out garden.*

Opposite: *A stunning bank of wisteria climbs a sheer rock-face.*

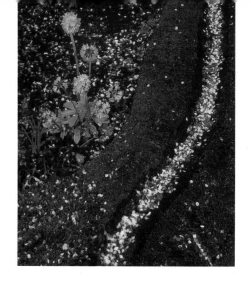

THE GARDEN OF

PRINCESS NICHOLAS ABKHAZI
VICTORIA, BRITISH COLUMBIA

I came to Victoria from Shanghai in 1945 after two and a half years of internment in a Japanese prisoner-of-war camp. When I first arrived, I often walked with friends through what were then fields to my present property. We would climb the large rock where my house is now situated and watch the sunset. I loved that rock; it seemed to have been there for ever and, after years of personal upheavals, it gave me a sense of security and permanency. When the property on which it stood was being subdivided, I was able to choose the long, thin strip of land that is now my garden.

It was at this time that I married, and my husband (also a former prisoner of war, in Germany) and I built a small summer house, which still stands on the property, and started to clear the land ourselves. In doing this, we were able to see what we

Top: *Rhododendron petals litter the ground.*

Right: *A view of the pond in spring.*

Opposite: *"The Yangtze River"—a hedge of heather.*

had bought and thus plan the garden. The house was built in due course on top of the rock. The garden curves around below it. Each year, as the garden progressed, my husband took slides which we studied in the winter, in order to correct our mistakes and make new plans.

Our first plantings were for a speedy show of colour and effect – daffodils, tulips, aubrieta, etc., but we gradually developed more permanent ideas – heathers, hybrid brooms, prostrate and upright blue spruces and other conifers. As the coppice of Garry oaks improved with the care they received, we thought how wonderful it would be to have a rhododendron wood, with the added pleasures of ferns, cyclamen, primroses, pleiones, etc. We got to know the famous nurserymen of Victoria (Layritz, Tohbrunner, Christiansen and Goddard), who gave us their rhododendron and azalea treasures, some of which were fairly tall and mature. So we had a good start, and over the years we concentrated on rhododendrons and azaleas, which flower between January and June, with a magnificent

Far and near left: The pond in early spring and a month later, when the marsh-marigolds and azaleas are in full bloom.

Opposite below: Hybrid broom stand out against an outcropping of rock.

Below: A carefully shaped mass of pink Japanese azaleas beside a footpath.

show in April and May. After this splendour I love the green of the trees, all shades of green from yellow to blue, providing interest even during the winter months.

When planning the garden I had a picture in my mind of the Yangtze River. There would be no sharp angles; it should curve on and on, flowing peacefully, everything circular. The Chinese way of gardening doesn't show or tell everything at once. It involves an arrangement of small "rooms" with the idea that one is continually going around curves to yet another garden.

There is a Chinese proverb which says that to be happy for a week you take a new concubine, to be happy for a month you kill a pig, and to be happy all your life you build a garden. I can't vouch for the first two, but the last is true.

Above: *A mass of azaleas in bloom.*

Right: *The rhododendron forest.*

Right: Fallen tulip petals scattered across a rock.

Far right: Purple aubrieta, bluebells and Helleborus orientalis *cascade down a slope.*

Below: Bergenia crassifolia *in bloom.*

THE GARDEN OF

RITA LEHMANN
VANCOUVER, BRITISH COLUMBIA

In the wet, mild climate here, it is possible to garden the year round. Shortly after moving here years ago, we built a greenhouse near the house and expanded the possibilities. I began to learn from friends, gardening courses at the University of British Columbia, massive reading and a lot of trial and error.

The garden, which slopes rather sharply from road to ocean level, consists of several rock gardens and a few flat areas. Three sets of steps descend through a group of three enormous fir trees, under which I have planted shrubs, native ferns and flowers. On the south face of one fir trunk a *Clematis montana rubens* climbs up and tumbles across the carport, making a spectacular show in April.

In a more open situation is the solar greenhouse we built to replace the old one. I do all my

propagating here; orchids, clivias, bougainvilleas, azaleas, geraniums, early tomatoes in pots, cucumbers in hanging baskets all share the space. In front of the greenhouse is one of several vegetable growing spots. Three raised beds contain the results of a winter-vegetable hobby. I seed Armado cauliflower and purple sprouting broccoli in mid-summer and harvest them the following February through April. Ordinary peas, beans, spinach, tomatoes and cucumbers grow here early in the season; leeks, kale, corn salad, onions and winter lettuce under cloches during the winter.

For visitors not enchanted by vegetables the huge blooms of the tree peonies nearby provide a magnificent distraction in May, as does the rest of the spring rock garden ablaze with rhododendrons, azaleas and dozens of rock-hugging plants of all shapes and colours.

Below the house, facing south to the sea, is another steep rocky slope and a flat area where an espaliered peach tree shares space with one climbing rose. Since this spot gets a lot of sun, some pockets of red and pink schizostylis bloom from mid-summer until frost. This dainty flower provides a constant supply of splendid material for Japanese flower arrangements.

The location of the garden is magnificent, but there are too many experiments going on for it to be a show place, well designed and always neat. But I hope it is an interesting and welcoming place.

Opposite: *A wall of azaleas and ericaceous plants leads down to the sea wall.*

Below: *Aubrieta nestles in the stone steps.*

Bottom: *Yellow alyssum tumble over the sea wall.*

THE GARDEN OF

JEANNIE SOUTHAM
VANCOUVER, BRITISH COLUMBIA

Spring usually comes early here, setting off the daffodil walk and, around the pond, the Japanese cherry, cut-leaf maple, *Magnolia stellata* and rhododendrons – peach, pearl and 'Hello Dolly'.

Later the yellow iris at the edges of the pond come into bloom. The water-lilies spread their pads, but don't bloom until summer – white, pale pink and a new yellow variety. The little English lead putto that my father gave us stands by the pond, waiting to see it all.

On the terrace by the house are many ivies housing nesting finches, and we have also nurtured a huge bougainvillea, which is taken down in the fall, twined around inside the greenhouse and then, in May or June, twined again around the posts of the terrace. People can't seem to believe it when they see it: after all, this is not Mexico!

The *Clematis montana* then blooms. It has now climbed through a huge old rhododendron into an enormous English oak tree. One or the other will have to go; but how could we make a decision like that? Fight it out, I say, hoping they will both survive.

An ivy-covered stump leads to a tree-house now thirty-five years old among the maple trees, and a new generation – our grandchildren – are finding it a splendid place to hide and avoid confrontations.

In front of our house are two knot gardens (copied from a picture in *House and Garden* magazine) on either side of a square raised brick bed which in the spring holds glorious pink Elizabeth Arden tulips rising through a thicket of blue pansies. During the summer they are replaced by 'Pink Camellia' geraniums. Inside the V's of the two knot gardens we plant dwarf pink dahlias.

We also have hedges of old and new rhododendrons, which seem to excel in this climate. They are every colour from white to mauve to pink to rose to coral to peach and lemon yellow – which sounds

Above: *Elizabeth Arden tulips dominate the knot garden in spring.*

Right: Cotoneaster *spreads over the bank of the pond.*

Opposite, above: *Espaliered English ivy against a bare wall.*

Opposite, below: *Summer bloom takes over a shady place where, in spring, a carpet of* Vinca minor, *ferns and lily of the valley thrives.*

awful, and maybe it is, but we love them anyhow.

Another part of the garden I love is the wild shady place between the neighbouring house and ours. A thick carpet of *Vinca minor* (periwinkle) is studded with large ferns from the woods as well as maidenhair and clumps of lily of the valley.

Growing tall through this are beautiful old dogwood trees, which were here when we arrived in 1950. Every spring when they bloom, I am happy and young all over again. I love this wild garden, this pond, this sunny terrace.

Right: An unusual, colourful planting of annuals at the foot of a tree.

Below: An extravagant display of Nelly Moser clematis among rhododendrons and colourful annuals.

Opposite: The Juan de Fuca Strait seen from the top of the garden.

THE GARDEN OF

JACK TODD
VICTORIA, BRITISH COLUMBIA

"Highcrest" is situated on top of a hill at the southernmost tip of Vancouver Island. The garden is made up of two different areas. The top of the property, ninety-three feet above sea level, has a 360° view of mountains and sea. It has full sun all day long but is subject to prevailing winds and winter storms. This area of natural rock formation is planted with alpines, ground-hugging plants, heathers and dwarf bonsai-like trees, and there are several ponds that are home to water-lilies, goldfish and *koi*. These ponds not only add to the beauty

of the garden but also attract many species of birds and butterflies, and a large patio sheltered by the house from the summer breezes offers a spectacular view.

From the upper garden on the north side are winding pathways and steps set into the contour of the hill. This route is planted with a variety of native ferns, bonsai pines and alpine plants, many of which have been collected on Vancouver Island. As you pass by a collection of bonsai trees in containers, you enter the lower garden, which is quite sheltered from the wind. Centred by a lawn of native grasses and native Garry oak trees, its perimeter is planted with rhododendrons, azaleas and some perennials which form a background for winding borders. In the spring these borders contain polyanthus, wallflowers, forget-me-nots, pansies and other spring plants together with plantings of spring bulbs, trilliums, etc. In summer these are replaced with summer annuals and hybrid lilies planted here and there. This is a garden of colour, and because of our mild climate, even in winter there is colour in the lower garden.

Gently sloping pathways and steps take you back to the top of the hill from the south-west side. As you reach the top a long pond comes into view and beyond it Mount Baker. Angling across the pond are a series of stepping stones leading to the highest point of the garden.

Thanks to quantities of soil and humus, what was twelve years ago a hill covered with Scotch broom and blackberry bushes now has a large variety of plants and shrubs. I hope we have created a garden of love and beauty without destroying the natural contour of the land.

Above: *Brilliant campanula swathe stone steps.*

Left: *Winding borders lead to the lower garden.*

THE GARDEN OF

SHIRLEY BEACH
VICTORIA, BRITISH COLUMBIA

When we bought our property in 1973, the only plant in the garden was a large clump of red peonies by the front steps. In many ways this was a good thing, since we could start from scratch.

My husband enjoys constructing paths, arches, pergolas, anything that I can sketch or at least describe; he leaves the planning and choice of plants to me. If there is a theme to our garden, it is that it should complement our late-Victorian house; it should be soft coloured, nothing harsh or strident.

We have a small, formal herb garden, but the roses have taken over everywhere else. As I read more and more gardening books, I became interested in old roses, and when I found a local nursery that imported some from England, we bought Mme Hardy, York and Lancaster, Old Blush

Above: *A close-up of the thyme lawn.*

Left: *The thyme lawn seen from above.*

Far left: *An overview of the garden from an upstairs window.*

Over: *A profusion of soft colours delights the eye and adds enchantment.*

China, Crested Moss (Chapeau de Napoléon) and *Rosa primula*. We were so happy with them that we ordered fifty more roses from England; they have been a joy ever since. Old roses are now available in Canada and we have added so many that the garden is full. We underplant them with as many dianthus, campanulas, hardy geraniums, iris, primroses, auriculas, *Vinca minor* and violas as we can accommodate. Among the climbing roses, we grow lots of

clematis, mostly mauve shades as well as several of the small-flowered species. As there is no more room left in the ground, we are turning to troughs to squeeze in a few more plants.

We in this part of Canada are very fortunate that we can enjoy the garden year round. In the winter there are hellebores, violets, primroses, cyclamen and winter jasmine. With spring come the bulbs, anemones, pulsatilla, more primroses, auriculas, early

clematis, and in May the first of the roses – *Rosa banksiae lutea* and *Rosa alba plena* – followed in high summer by all the lovely old roses.

People tell me the garden smells heavenly, but, sad to say, I am in it so much of the time I don't notice the fragrance as much as visitors do.

Above: *Leverkusen, one of many old-fashioned roses.*

Opposite: *A rustic arch supports climbing roses and clematis.*

Right: A native wild rose.

Below: A sculptural boulder shelters hand-planted cow parsley.

Opposite: A freshly mown old buffalo trail.

Over: A profusion of peonies lines the trail to an old slough.

THE GARDEN OF

MARY DOVER
MIDNAPORE, ALBERTA

When I bought it in the late 1950s, this land was part of a cow pasture, virgin land which had never been cultivated. Chief David Crowchild fenced it for me and gave it its name: "Oksi" is a Blackfoot word meaning "a good place." For centuries, wood buffalo, deer and moose had lived in these hills, and their tracks had worn permanent paths through fields and woods to an old slough. As I walked these paths, I discovered white and blue wood violets, wintergreen and shooting stars, twin flowers, baneberries, wild cranberries and raspberries, grass of Parnassus and orchids. My

garden was already there – in adding to it, I wanted most of all to keep its wildness.

Wherever the land sloped to the south, Chinook winds had prevented trees and shrubs from growing, so I brought in crab apples, Siberian pears, lilacs, honeysuckles, shrub roses and a triple line of one hundred vivid peonies.

After that, I journeyed to gardens in Britain, Italy and Japan. At home, the books of famous gardeners filled my shelves and set me dreaming. One dream was to protect from predators the wild ducks, Canada geese and water-loving fowl who summered with me every year. In this I hope I have succeeded.

I have started an arboretum and already there are willows, large spruce, Douglas fir, several varieties of pines and junipers. Native choke cherries, saskatoons, mock oranges and the exquisite wild pale-blue climbing clematis grow in the shade. Alberta is known for its wild roses and these are at Oksi Hill in profusion and perfection. Lately, having discovered the hybridists' success with the hardy Explorer rose series, I have planted some. Unfortunately the unmannerly mule deer consider them a gourmet treat.

There is little formality in my garden. Near the house there are a few flowerbeds, and a shaded grassy place which is pleasant for tea; beyond is a sunken garden made to clear away a mosquito haunt. The garden may one day be of horticultural interest. At present, it is a place of beauty and profound peace, strangely touching the many visitors who come to explore it.

Above: *This raised wooden walkway winds through a bog full of iris and native plants.*

Far left: *Broad swatches of roughly mown trails surround the dried-up slough in summer.*

Left: *A Philadelphus 'Waterton', particular to Waterton Lakes in Southern Alberta, planted in a natural stand of aspen.*

Below: A casually planted perennial border near the house.

Right: Pulsatilla gone to seed in front of a mass of aquilegia.

THE GARDEN OF

MARY TALBOT
MEANOOK, ALBERTA

I have always liked gardening so when, some years ago, I was left with one and a half acres, several goats and a small flock of poultry, I soon decided that I did not want to be bothered with livestock but would rather spend more time gardening. The animals went and the paraphernalia of hay bales and wire pens were cleared up. As I no longer needed a large vegetable garden, I planted more flowers. When I ran out of space, I moved the annual vegetables to a more open spot, leaving the perennial herbs and small fruits in what was

Below: *A border of blue* Veronica austriaca, *mauve* penstemon, *Alberta native yellow daisies and white* Silene maritima.

Over: *A tapestry of bloom dominated by yellow sedum, blue and purple* Veronica spicata *and* Dianthus arenarius.

to become a kind of cottage garden, a medley of small shrubs, herbaceous perennials and bulbs, all ornamental and some edible.

I grew up in England, and so have been influenced by the borders and naturalistic style of gardens there. I don't, however, think of my present garden as English, but rather as Albertan, shaped by local conditions and an integral part of the surrounding hayfields and woods of this little valley. Poplar, choke cherry, wild rose and hazel grow along the south boundary of the land, and small areas of natural bush have been left within.

The choice of exotic trees and shrubs is limited in this rather severe climate with its long, cold winter and short growing season, but I wanted to try as many herbaceous perennials as I could get. Not many plants were available locally so I joined some plant societies, chiefly to take advantage of their seed lists but also to learn more about growing things.

As the number of plants increased, I dug more ground and widened existing beds in order to find homes for them. Generally, I prefer the simpler wild flowers and species to the showier but often more demanding hybrids and cultivars. My garden is not tidy. I like the plants to seed themselves around, for then, I feel, they are truly at home.

Left: *Blue* Veronica austriaca *and* Veronica latifolia *and* Rosa altaica *(native Siberian rose) line a gravel walk.*

THE GARDEN OF

BILL AND ANNE PETERS
CRESTON, BRITISH COLUMBIA

We created our gardens on five acres of rough bushland surrounded by orchards, and the effect, we hope, is a pleasant walk through a series of different gardens and views. Upon entering, one passes through a grove of flowering crab apples, the path lined with flower borders. The path crosses a natural creek and climbs a steep incline through a rock garden, then a grove of native birch. Planted and sheltered among the birch is our collection of rhododendrons, which give a beautiful showing every spring.

Coming back into the sunshine, the path meanders through lily beds and around small shrubs and trees. It leads into an enclosed area, designed by our friend Graham Brown, which features an azalea border, a large fish pond, trees and a long perennial border. A rose trellis connects this to the rose garden, which contains beds

Above: An arbour covered with Blaze roses.

Left: The Rocky Mountains form a majestic backdrop for the hybrid tea rose garden.

of nearly two hundred hybrid tea roses. The centre of the garden is at the highest point of our land, where one gets a spectacular view of the surrounding mountains and valley.

From here the gardens slope downward two hundred feet to the crest of the creek valley. Part way down is a stone cairn which is the source of a man-made brook. This winds its way down the slope, tumbling over little falls, passing under a red arched footbridge and ending up in a pool at the foot of the garden. The path descends to the creek and across another little bridge, then back to the shadehouse at the entrance to the garden.

Our gardens change with the seasons. After the spring flowers, the perennial beds begin to show colour early, and the lilies put on a vibrant display of bright oranges and yellows through late June and July. The roses and annual flowers keep the colours high all through the summer, and as fall comes on, the leaves turn various shades of red, yellow and orange, a last burst of colour before the quiet of winter.

The gardens have been a labour of love on our part, but we could never have succeeded in developing them without the substantial help of family and friends. Some of them must have questioned our sanity during the early years when the area was just bush and rough land; now, twenty years later, they can see the fruits of our labours.

Top: The greens of hostas and weeping birch are accentuated by plantings of brightly coloured annuals.

Above: A stand of young birch near the pond.

Left: Tall cedars shelter a perennial bed that includes aquilegia, dianthus, coreopsis and lupin.

THE GARDEN OF

SUSAN McCUTCHEON
TORONTO, ONTARIO

Above: *The sculpture of birds at the centre of the terrace creates an ever-changing shadow on the pond.*

Below: *The fountain of birds dramatizes this apartment balcony garden.*

I moved to this apartment because of the deck, which dominates the entire eastern wall, which is all glass. There is an exit from each bordering interior room. Other than the original cedar decking and a few juniper bushes, the space was untouched when I arrived. The garden that was created is the inspired work of a number of people. Brad Johnson and Philip Weinstein of Johnson, Sustronk, Weinstein gave me wonderful design advice. And through them I met Ron Baird, the sculptor who made the magnificent fountain birds and other pieces for me.

The whole project took about a year to complete. The space was divided into four areas, each one designed to relate to its contiguous interior room, so that areas outside the living- and dining-rooms are quite open and public, while those next to the bedrooms are more concealed and private.

The plant material we had chosen arrived all together one magical spring day and was planted as quickly as possible. As the maximum soil depth is eighteen inches, water drains away quickly and must be replenished more frequently than in gardens with more sub-soil. Although an automatic watering system is in place, I have always preferred to water the garden by hand. The time it takes – an hour a day or so if it's hot and dry – is a wonderful break and gives me the opportunity to become familiar with the plants.

Each season brings new shapes and colours of leaves, bark and berries. The constantly changing scenery dominates my living space – in fact, I live in my garden!

Above: *A screen of textured greens lends intimacy to the terrace.*

Left: *A secluded area outside a bedroom.*

Right: *Rain-soaked peonies droop over alium gone to seed.*

Below: *A wide variety of white and silver flowers and plants creates the mood of this garden.*

Opposite: *An overview of the enclosed quiet garden.*

THE GARDEN OF

PATRICK LIMA AND JOHN SCANLAN
MILLER LAKE, ONTARIO

When we moved from Toronto to the rocky Bruce Peninsula in 1975, our intention was simply to grow an extended organic food garden – vegetables, fruit and culinary herbs. Inevitably, however, we soon branched out, most enthusiastically into flower growing.

Our garden is flat and sun filled, a former hayfield left to its own wild ways for several decades. Clearing garden space was (and still is) done with spade, fork and rake. We fertilize with quantities of organic matter – truck-loads of decayed cow manure, sacks of maple leaves and lots of compost.

From the start we resolved to furnish the garden with plants suited to site, soil and climate. Frost may strike here as late as June 10th and again by the first week in September. Taking our clues from several treasured old gardening books, we began to

explore the world of hardy herbaceous perennials and alpine plants.

Our garden, Larkwhistle, was not planned in total from the start. As an example, the area we now call the "main flower garden" began as a single 10-foot x 75-foot raised border planted first with potatoes, then with annual flowers and finally with perennials. Across the path from this border we dug a parallel 5-foot-wide bed for daffodils, bearded irises, peonies, pinks and other flowers. This arrangement suggested another 10-foot-wide border across the way to balance the first. With an enclosing fence of salvaged cedar rails, an entrance arbour and gate, a vine-draped bower and benches, one "garden room" took its present shape. In this space we look for successive waves of colour from the time the first wild spring crocus opens until the showy fall sedum mellows to autumn brown.

Inspiration for our work comes from many sources – the plants themselves, books and other gardens. A bicycle tour of English gardens inspired Larkwhistle's most recent "room" – a "quiet garden" where the silver leaves of sea lyme grass, hostas and lamb's ears make a cool setting for white-flowered campanulas, heucheras, Madonna lilies, delphiniums, roses, phlox and creamy *Artemisia lactiflora.*

Left, top: *In late June and early July, masses of dianthus, lilies and peonies dominate the centre border of the main garden.*

Left, middle: *Peonies, roses and iris flank a cedar rail fence.*

Left, bottom: *Oriental poppies (Perry's White) rise above silver* Stachys lanata *and pink dianthus.*

Opposite: *The main garden when the peonies are at their peak.*

Throughout the flower gardens we try to combine colours for harmonious "living pictures." For example, a rosy border flanking the vegetable garden shows a consistent scheme of crimson, pink, lavender, mauve and blue (no yellows, orange or scarlet) from mid-May to September.

The garden also yields fresh vegetables from May to November, an array of herbs for cooking and succulent pesticide-free fruit. We can only be grateful. A definition of a garden that we read years ago in *My Garden* by Louise Beebe Wilder has proven apt: A garden, she says, is "a spot converted from the common land and made intimate and personal, sacred to beauty and sweetness, to delightful work and quiet meditation."

Left: *A close-up view of the "rosy border."*

THE GARDEN OF

BARBARA FRUM
DON MILLS, ONTARIO

I am a relative newcomer to gardening and so my garden, like my life, is a work in progress, with many unresolved patches awaiting creative inspiration. I had been the relaxed custodian of a fairly routine suburban backyard until the mania struck about five years ago. But what's been clear from the day I decided the backyard should be a garden is that, all along, I was destined for this affliction.

Now that I'm an addict, a spade won't do. When I take on a garden project, it requires earth-moving equipment, tons of fresh soil, full-grown trees and bushes dropped in by crane.

I think of gardens as the place for the bold stroke, the indulgence of whim, with all the inherent risks of folly. I've made my own an austere composition in brown and green. Above all I care about the contour of land, about vistas, and about the form and placement of plants. I prefer a bank of moss and thyme and river-washed pebbles to an immaculate bed of perfect

tulips. Bark and foliage move me more than a smartly clipped hedge or a splendid perennial border. I love blooms and blossoms, of course, and fragrance is a precious bonus, but my main goal is a landscape that's beautiful in all seasons, in the rain, under snow, in the sodden mists of March and in the sweet, sad, lavender light of late November.

To look good all year, a garden needs great bones. In my garden the structure comes from an undulating shallow valley with pine trees along its length, and from some creaky but elegant old black locusts which put out a frothy canopy of fronds each summer that dapples light down onto the woodland floor below.

It's my belief that the gardener is invariably a relentless, obsessive

Above: *Different hues of green are the theme of this subtly conceived garden.*

Left: *An austere composition of brown and green.*

perfectionist, forever on the move
across the landscape in a bent-
over posture. Your visitor sees
beauty and showers praise and
encouragement. You see only
mistakes to be corrected which, of
course, is precisely what keeps you
hooked.

Gardening for me is not about
success or about contentment. It's
about our struggle against time,
about anticipation, and never-
ending hope, followed inevitably
by frustration and disappoint-
ment, with just enough triumph
to keep the addiction fed.

Opposite, above: *A textured glade of hostas, ferns, bark and foliage.*

Opposite, below: *In a corner, a carpet of mixed sedums under pine and spruce.*

Above: *A reclining statue and dwarf Japanese maple dominate a small garden room near the house.*

Left: *Native phlox adds colour to this miniature landscape.*

THE GARDEN OF

HARVEY SOBEL
HAMILTON, ONTARIO

Top: *An apple tree in spring blossom.*

Above: *A statue of Hermes at the back of the garden.*

Right: *The garden in summer.*

My day begins and ends in the sanctuary of my garden. Even in winter the evergreens and cardinals create an incredible landscape.

Southwest Hamilton is built on red clay, so only a rose garden would do extremely well here. To eliminate this problem, the first step was to remove four feet of clay and replace it with black loam to enable rhododendrons, azaleas, dogwood and other plants to flourish. At the time, the cost seemed outrageous: I had paid $10,000 for the house; the loam was over $4,000. However, when I consider the more than twenty years of pleasure the garden has given me, it has indeed been a fine investment.

I wanted a garden with little or no maintenance and one that would combine a small formal

garden with a natural setting. On a lot 50 feet by 120 feet, this required careful planning.

Having a laneway behind the property allowed me to plant hepaticas, pink and white trilliums, wild ferns, snowdrops and lilies that give pleasure to my neighbours as well as myself.

We have two courtyards and a raised area with a gazebo, as well as the central formal area with a fountain made from an eighteenth-century tole roof finial.

The rather grotesque terracotta

benches in the formal area were found in Vincenza. I remember thinking how truly gross they were, and deciding that if they gave me a chuckle that day they had more amusement in store.

I once heard a sermon describing the instant creation of a mature garden, using cranes, bulldozers and the planting of forty-foot trees. The rabbi, after a long explanation, ended his sermon by saying, "Can you imagine what God would have done if he'd had the money?"

The essence of a beautiful

garden has to be the essence of life. With understanding, care and love your garden rewards you in return.

Above: A walkway lined with ferns and tulips leads to a secluded corner of the garden.

Opposite: The view towards the house.

THE GARDEN OF

EVELYN LAMBART

SUTTON, QUÉBEC

When I first saw this property in 1969, it was an abandoned pasture, a tangle of brambles, thorns, alder, elder and poplar, with many wild apples and some maples – really rather bleak. But it also had natural rock outcroppings, springs, a bog and a view extending a total of thirty-five miles. I bought it.

I immediately employed a forester who removed most of the offending growth, put in drainage ditches, made the bog into a pond, put in a shelter belt of pine

Top: *Cobweb house leek grows out of a rock crevice.*

Above and opposite: *Beds of* Alchemilla mollis, *coneflowers, lilies and coreopsis form a corner of the hillside border.*

and spruce and said, "Taste the apples, mark the ones you like and I'll take the rest." Today, I consider these apples nicer than anything I can buy. Each tree is different and each new tree as it comes into bearing is different again. There is even one with a coffee flavour, which I hope to spread around by grafting this spring.

Planning a garden on paper has never worked for me. I had to visualize what I wanted, starting with the entrance to the land and working out from there. One thing I knew was that I was more interested in a few good flower specimens set off against a texture of green foliage than in masses of ordinary "ever-blooming" plants.

A lot of the ground here is very steep with only a thin layer of soil over the bed-rock but with lots of lovely green stones in it. The natural thing was to build terraces of the rock and to back-fill. This has developed into a wonderful place to grow and display plants; some hang on the edge, some get their roots under the next tier of stone at the back and others spread out carpet-like. As I expose more of the rock, I experiment to find the right plants for the right spot. They all get good exposure to light and nothing is hidden from view.

I use duck manure to back-fill and also to mulch well; it keeps down the weeds. I use several tons a year which I spread myself. There is very little hand weeding to do, and I use almost no fertilizer.

Left: A vertical planting of dianthus, ferns and mosses enhances the lines of a cathedral like rock outcropping.

Apart from the pleasure of working the garden, there are all the intelligent, warm-hearted, generous, sincere people you can't help but meet and the great pleasure of exchanging treasures with them. I feel as rooted here as the plants. I hate leaving the place. This is where I want to be and this is what I want to do.

Top: *An interesting combination of ornamental grasses and orange dahlias among the rocks.*

Above: Yellow *Sedum acre follows the horizontal contours of a rock-face.*

Left: *Man-made fieldstone terraces show off a fine display of specimen plants.*

THE GARDEN OF

MARGARET CLARKE

HUDSON, QUÉBEC

My great-great-grandfather bought Sydenham Cottage in 1836 – a wedding present to his daughter and her new husband. The young couple planned the original garden with a lawn of three flat terraces, a large round central flowerbed, and a lilac hedge beside the driveway. The customary vegetable and small fruits garden was beside the kitchen. But their real love was obviously for trees, because they planted a great many, some of which still stand.

Succeeding generations have each left their mark. Two of my sisters and an aunt made the greatest alterations. They began by moving the vegetable garden away from the house, across the small stream which now divides the gardens. Along its banks they began a rock garden, and on the nearer side of the lawn they planned the present rectangular perennial and rose garden.

The perennial borders have always been a mixture of native and cultivated varieties. Wild lupins from Cape Breton, polemonium from Kentucky woods, bergenia from the Orkneys, St Joseph's lily from Québec's Eastern Townships, and others gathered from here and there mix happily with Shasta daisies, phlox, delphiniums, day lilies, bergamot and Canterbury bells.

I used to enjoy the early tulips and crocuses in the rock garden, but an invasion of black squirrels ate them all, so I've now replaced them with primulas – my real spring favourites and unattractive to wildlife. *Primula juliae* is the earliest to bloom, followed by *Primula denticulata*, then *sieboldii* and *japonica*. Other plants emerge among them – bloodroot, hepaticas, blue flax, red and yellow columbines and others from the woods, along with aubrieta, arabis, geums, *Iris cristata*, cranesbill, campanula (harebells) and so on.

I've used other people's ideas quite shamelessly. Native low-growing evergreens, ferns and bergenia now fill in shady spaces and provide background where necessary. A visit to Sissinghurst in Kent suggested the use of bush roses like Harison's Yellow as a natural trellis for clematis. Andromeda Gardens in Barbados inspired me to make my own garden tiles from cement, with leaf patterns pressed into the wet surfaces. Some of my ideas have worked and some have definitely not. I continue to make mistakes and try something else. That's half the fun.

Above: *These borders are a mixture of native and cultivated plants.*

Above right: *A close-up of daisies and heuchera.*

Right: *A small stream planted with moisture-loving plants divides the garden.*

Far right: *Clematis montana climbs a tree by the porch.*

THE GARDEN OF

NICOLE EATON
GEORGIAN BAY, ONTARIO

Above: *An aerial view of the vegetable and herb gardens.*

Right: *Soil had to be brought in by barge to create this raised vegetable garden on a windswept rock-face.*

Each spring, after an absence of six or eight months, I arrive back at Little Jane Island in Georgian Bay full of dread to see what the bears and beavers have nibbled, trampled or simply done away with altogether.

The perennial bed, behind a stone retaining wall, overhangs the water by the main dock. It is one of the few patches of earth on the island. The border is one big square divided by 350 day lilies into four smaller squares containing digitalis, verbascum, blue monarda, Black Dragon and Madonna lilies, delphinium, achilleas, campanula, thalictrum and masses of phlox for August.

Page 106

Right: *Delphiniums in bloom in high summer.*

Below: *Astilbe and other shade-loving plants nestle in the crevices of the rock.*

My children sow green and pink zinneas and cosmos to fill in the holes. Not subtle or botanically exotic, perhaps, but a lavish and exuberant display of bloom and colour which I cut and arrange into bouquets with other odd plants I find in amongst the rocks. The fragrance of the flowers, drifting through the house on the breezes off the water, is wonderful.

The plantings on both sides of the path leading to the house are shaded by pines and birches. A massive rock fall on one side lends architectural interest. Expeditions to neighbouring islands for mosses, ferns and woodland plants, a massing of white astilbe and a growing collection of hostas make this a tranquil space.

The first ripe tomato of the season reminds me that Little Jane's vegetable and herb garden are a triumph of greed over nature. The three small beds are built on a flat rock with a retaining wall two stones deep along all four sides. I have planted hybrid teas amongst the herbs and have broken the beds into tri-angles, using lavender, parsley, chives and basil as edging.

Across the bay I have tucked varieties of rugosa, musk and hybrid perpetual roses amongst the boulders of the shoreline. They have survived the winter, which encourages my foolhardiness to plant more.

Little Jane is not my ideal place for a garden. I like symmetry, classical statuary, hedges and vistas. However, the challenge of working within the rugged contours of rock and water have been very rewarding. I can already imagine an enlarged herb garden, I can smell the antique roses across the way and I can anticipate several winter evenings reading next season's seed catalogues.

Right: *A sweeping stone wall encloses the perennial beds featuring delphiniums, which are followed by day lilies and other summer perennials.*

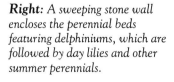

Above: *Multi-layered, multi-textured planting adds a sense of space to this very small city garden.*

Right: *A striking alium stands out against a plain garden fence.*

Far right: *Trellised architectural features and a gazebo give the garden style and grandeur.*

THE GARDEN OF

AL CUMMINGS
TORONTO, ONTARIO

"It's a nice house," said friends. "Too bad it doesn't have a garden." Behind the house I had purchased in Toronto stood a crumbling stucco garage with an expanse of ruptured concrete leading up to it. It was difficult to imagine that anything could be made of such an unpromising space – even if the garage were demolished.

Still, I asked my friend and landscape architect Tom Sparling to look at the property and make suggestions. My goal was to create an attractive outdoor area for my own use and a separate area for the family that occupies the first-floor apartment of the house, and provide parking space for two cars.

Tom came back with a plan that accomplished everything I had hoped for and more. It retained only one old lilac bush wedged in the corner of the garden; Tom imagined it arching over a fountain and small pool. A gate from an enclosed tenant's garden could be opened for a view of the fountain or closed for privacy.

After the garage had been demolished, the ground was levelled and grey lattice-topped fencing installed to enclose the entire space. A pergola was built

to make the entrance to my garden area. Brickwork and flower beds were laid down inside the two gardens.

Four full-grown honey locust trees were installed in the garden to provide dappled shade. Landscape gardener Robert Brown supervised the planting of flowering shrubs and vines, perennials and ground cover. From a colourful display of spring bulbs to a handsome mix of perennials and annuals in summer, the planting in the garden was designed to give colour over a period of months without requiring constant maintenance.

I have never missed the garage, and I think the garden is proof that even within a small urban backyard it is possible to create a space that is both beautiful and useable for outdoor living.

THE GARDEN OF

THÉRÈSE ROMER DE BELLEFEUILLE
ST-EUSTACHE, QUÉBEC

Top: Tree peonies blossom above myosotis.

Above: *Siberian irises border the river at St-Eustache.*

Opposite: *Drifts of yellow day lilies and lilac-coloured* Hesperis *'Dame's Violet' or 'Sweet Rocket' fill casually placed perennial borders.*

My husband's family has old ties with this traditional Québec village where, in 1972, we discovered our rambling, historic house with its lovely setting of trees and lawn sloping to the river. I added drifts of hesperis, shrub roses, all the lovely old standbys, and have experimented with unusual varieties, here at the edge of hardiness: *Magnolia stellata, Fritillaria persica,* colchicum species. But I am especially fond of our native species – trilliums, tiarellas, sanguinarias and many others.

Winter brings some of this garden's most spectacular flowerings – fleeting, breath-catching, none of our doing – as each fresh snowfall sets off the lacework of

Above: *Ground elder,*
Anemone canadensis and
spirea flourish together in a shady
corner.

Right: *A carpet of lily of the*
valley.

Far right: *The branches of a*
tree dance against a green
backdrop.

branches against an ultramarine sky. After a late spring, our quick, lush, colourful summer – full of annuals and perennials and shady retreats amid trees and ferns – bears comparison with anything the tropics has to offer. Fall, however, is for me the year's high point, with its explosion of Indian summer, awash in fiery oranges, reds and yellows.

I guess I'm more plantswoman than garden planner, never having brought myself, despite exhortations, to work with pencil and squared paper. I'm given to on-site trial and error. Playing with shapes and colours, working the soil with (not against) nature have taught me to prize gardening as a bastion of fantasy, where true amateurs can still flourish without falling prey to rules or rampant professionalism.

An early convert to Ruth Stout, I've learned to value the benefits of organic growing. This one-and-a-half-acre garden is wholly looked after by two women, myself and a devoted neighbour, so we rely on mulches, sheet composting, no-dig and green-thumb-without-an-aching-back methods. Vegetables, I sadly confess, get rather short shrift, though a few tomatoes, snowpeas and herbs are indispensable, as is the raspberry patch.

Nothing would please me better than to garden full-time, yet the demands of home and job have had to take precedence. I'd love to have a well-appointed garden, but have to be content with a happy-go-lucky one, counting my blessings and thanking God for letting me live in close touch with this rainbow of delights.

THE GARDEN OF

TOM AND JOYCE MULOCK
NEWMARKET, ONTARIO

Our garden consists of fifteen acres of lawns, trees and shrubs casually combined. The hundred or so varieties of trees and shrubs, most of them planted ninety years ago by my husband's great-grandfather, Sir William Mulock, are grouped in loose masses around open lawns. Giant Norway spruce soaring ninety feet high are skilfully planted along tiered banks.

Beyond forty-foot-tall cedar hedges, a variety of fruit trees have been planted in clusters, thus creating a lovely balance of blossoms in the spring. Groves of black English walnut, a rare Romanian walnut presented to Sir William in 1900 by the Romanian government, oak and chestnut, red and white maple, Koster blue spruce, several elm beginning to reappear, mountain ash, flowering crab apple and almond, and forsythia are a sampling of the many species existing today.

Ornamental evergreens – pyramid cedar, mugho pine, spreading yew, privet, juniper and many others – are set where their silhouettes are clearly visible.

With each season the panorama changes. From spring to summer there is the enormous satisfaction of seeing the buds and young leaves making their first appearance, and the solitude of neighbouring woodland covered in a blanket of trilliums. In autumn the colours of the leaves range from pale yellow to burnt orange. In winter the evergreens provide a never-ending source of pride.

My husband and I have inherited a small but prodigious piece of Ontario, and we felt the best memorial we could offer was to continue living here, to replace the trees and shrubs that have perished and to maintain the property in the way its original owner envisaged it.

Opposite, above left and right: *Ancient trees and vast expanses of lawn are the main features of this old Ontario farm property.*

Opposite, below: *Thousands of trillium carpet the woods in May.*

Above: *A grove of rare English walnut trees.*

This garden is a continuation of our lifelong interest in flowers and gardens, especially in alpines and rock plants. It was started in the spring of 1977, following retirement from the harsh climate of northwestern Québec into the softer environment of the part of Ontario where we had spent our youth.

In our search for a natural rocky area to make a garden, we were fortunate in meeting Elgin and Mary Smith. At their farm several miles from our home, we found a small abandoned limestone quarry where early settlers had obtained stone for barn and house foundations, leaving behind the rougher capstone pieces. We were intrigued by the possibilities of using the quarry as our "garden" and discussed the project with Elgin Smith. He was not interested in selling or even leasing the area to us but encouraged us to make use of the land. The resulting friendship with Elgin and Mary and their family over the years remains a rich part of our retirement life.

We produce a succession of bloom from March to November, using only perennials. The season starts with blooms on the tufty cushions of the *Saxifraga porophylla*, followed by early bulbs. The great majority of rock plants are spring bloomers, and by mid-May the garden yields its peak of colour. Summer months are more subdued, but another burst of colour from later bloomers and second-time bloomers continues until freeze-up.

Rock gardening has given us an absorbing recreational vocation. Through memberships in alpine and rock garden societies we have obtained seeds of rare species not otherwise available, and have made many good friends among other enthusiasts with whom we share our gardens and experiences. Highlights each year include attending field trips to the mountains and garden visits with our confreres all over Canada and the United States.

THE GARDEN OF

CYRIL AND MARY BAKER
BRANTFORD, ONTARIO

Above: *White and pink arabis flank brilliant primula.*

Left: *Perennial* Alyssum saxatile, aubrieta *and* dianthus *tumble over the remains of an old quarry wall.*

Right: *The surrounding woods provide a peaceful backdrop to the tapestry of colour in the garden.*

The sweeping flower beds,
planted with alpine treasures,
follow the lines of the old quarry.

120

Above: Apple blossoms and spring bulbs contrast with the green formality of this city garden.

Right: New Dawn roses by the house.

Far right: The massing of standard hydrangea adds colour in late summer and fall.

THE GARDEN OF

HILARY WESTON
TORONTO, ONTARIO

When we moved here in 1976, nothing remained of the original garden except the remnants of a sunken rose garden and some very fine maple and lime trees. A visit to Vita Sackville-West's garden at Sissinghurst overwhelmed me; I became fascinated by the idea of garden rooms enclosed by clipped hedges, decorated with tumbling roses and patterned with flowers and shrubs, and above all, by my first sight of the famous white garden.

I returned to Canada determined to emulate in some way what I had seen at Sissinghurst. The sunken rose garden became a tennis court, and what remained became a room enclosed by cedar walls and patterned with boxwood and yew trees, the dominant colours green and white.

Having developed the framework, I then divided the space into a series of gravel and limestone pathways leading to a fountain garden, a pair of knot gardens planted in the seventeenth-century manner and a sculpture garden surrounded by a curving cedar hedge. My large trees remained, much against the advice of more worldly gardeners, and I succeeded in creating a woodland border underneath them.

By the terrace, two large borders of cream and white roses, with every variety that grows in this climate, produce an abundance of bouquets throughout the house and a sensational show outside until October.

My white garden is in constant evolution and I have now introduced some colour to it. The knot gardens are filled with magenta and pink primula, tradescantia, campanula and dianthus. After

Above: *A much-loved statue of Apollo.*

visiting Hatfield House in England, I intend to include varieties of pink roses.

I have tried to plant in my garden room elements that remind me of a childhood in Ireland: drifts of *Narcissus poeticus* inter-planted with vinca, apple blossoms in the springtime, rose-covered walls, the formality of the Irish yew and boxwood, an abundance of hydrangea in August, later to be dried and used to decorate the house and tree at Christmastime. I find the symmetry of the design calming and the green of the plantings a refuge from the summer heat. This garden truly satisfies my memories, while at the same time creating its own unique atmosphere, far from the wilds of County Wicklow.

Above: *Potted datura summering out, espaliered pear and standardized lilacs frame a garden gate.*

Left: *The sculpture garden.*

THE GARDEN OF

AMY AND CLAIR STEWART
CALEDON, ONTARIO

Opposite: Walls of local Caledon stone frame small garden enclosures.

Below left: A stand of sumac, brilliant in fall, is the buffer between the cultivated garden and the surrounding wilderness.

Below right: A folly made out of barn beams supports autumn clematis and gives shelter to tender plants.

In the 1950s, attracted by the open rolling pastures which offered a wide view to the south-east, we bought five hundred acres of abandoned farmland in the Albion Hills north-west of Toronto. The deep ravines that cut through the property still sheltered a variety of trees from the original forest, and we covered the bare fields with pine seedlings (100,000 over five years) which now form solid blocks of green, framing the valley and restricting the view. In the recent thinning process they supplied a reservoir of invaluable wood chips as mulch for our sandy garden soil.

Although we feel that a country garden should settle easily into the surrounding landscape, we planted a strip of manicured lawn to serve as a buffer between the house and the rough slope below it. And Clair has worked out a well-defined series of stone walls, terraces and broad steps descending the hill to a grass promontory which overlooks three trout ponds in the middle distance. A stream trickles over boulders into descending rock pools and loses itself in a marsh at the foot of the garden where water-loving plants now flourish. For architectural interest we

created our version of a garden folly modelled after a ruined barn foundation, complete with ancient beams.

Luxuriant alchemillas, berge-nias, stachys, hardy geraniums and the like soften the giant steps and carpet the hill. Plantings of coarse perennials – yarrow, knap-weed, globe thistle and rugosa roses – blur the line between garden and meadow. On a sandy sunbaked hill most bulbs (if not carried off by chipmunks) increase, and we have planted many thousands. Phlox, salvia, boltonia, asters and other late perennials find shelter within and

below the barn foundation.

It is not a showy garden There are no perennial borders, nor, with the exceptions of May when the hills are yellow with daffodils and September when the gold-enrod takes over, are there great drifts of colour to excite the imagi-nation. This is a casual country garden with a collection of plants that interest us. Its beauty depends to a large extent on the natural contours of the valley embraced by the forest; its strength lies in the central axis that draws the eye to the distant ponds.

The longer we live here, the more we appreciate the wider, wilder aspects of the valley, and it is our self-appointed task to settle the garden ever more comfortably into the landscape.

Above: *Asters grow among a mass of goldenrod.*

Left: *One of the three linked ponds that create a magnificent vista from the house.*

Far left: *Trellised honeysuckle tumble over a side perennial garden.*

Left: *Pansies add colour at the side of the house.*

THE GARDEN OF

REBECCA SIMARD
POINTE AU PIC, QUÉBEC

We bought our house on a hill overlooking the St Lawrence because of the garden. There was a certain wildness about it that I liked, and yet much of it has originally been designed to be formal and symmetrical.

It is always such a treat to spend time seeing what new flowers are blooming and making arrangements that change from week to week, from the pastel colours of spring to the rich, vibrant, darker colours of the fall.

I am fortunate that there is good soil here, and the garden is very sheltered because it is built into a hillside with fruit trees giving added protection. I have always loved flowers and particularly flower arranging, and I have been blessed with an abundance

of flowers that survive the harsh Québec winters here. They continue to bloom until the first frost. One thing that delights me is the surprise of seeing a flower that we did not plant growing in an unusual spot – a rock crevice or the vegetable garden.

When we rebuilt the old stone retaining walls of the flowerbeds, I had a great deal of help from Frank Cabot, a horticultural expert with an extraordinary eye. I learned from him that in addition to the larger planting, the garden should contain small surprises that just catch the eye rather than jump out at you.

My favourite part of the garden is along one side of the house. In mid-summer, the flowerbed here is ablaze with hundreds of pale pink

Left: The main garden is built into a hill with old stone retaining walls.

Bottom left: A massive spirea punctuates a corner of the garden.

Below: Mauve veronica dominates this perennial bed.

to hot pink phlox set against the Wedgwood blue of the house, with white trellises against the walls where orange honeysuckle climb. Splashes of orange lilies sprout up here and there. This year I am adding a cutting garden and am also going to play around with lilies to see what they do.

It has given me great joy to see how my garden has inspired friends to create their own, whether on a balcony in the city or on a farm in the country. Each garden seems to me to be a small paradise, the kind that only nature can offer.

THE GARDEN OF

FRANCIS CABOT
LA MALBAIE, QUÉBEC

Despite the fact that I had spent a good part of every summer of my life at "Les Quatre Vents," it was not until my wife and I became the owners of the property and had been exposed in our travels to the great gardens of the United Kingdom that I realized we had something with real horticultural promise on our hands.

We were fortunate in many respects. There was ample land and no end of views, with the Laurentians to the west, the St Lawrence to the east and the long headland of Pointe au Pic to the south. There was a typical northern maritime climate with its fogs, cool summer evenings, copious rains and deep winter snow cover. There was also an adequate supply of water in a stream that ran the year round along one edge of the garden. However, the most important

Far left: *The white garden contains a collection of summer-flowering plants, including such unusual specimens as white willow, autumn gentian,* Astrantia major, *black snake-root and* Campanula latifolia alba.

Middle left: *An old bread oven stands beside the topiary garden.*

Near left: *All the garden rooms in this large and varied garden are accessible from the Tapis Vert by the main house.*

Below: *A small pink garden of roses underplanted with dianthus leads off the Tapis Vert.*

factor was that the garden had been laid out in the 1930s by an uncle, Edward Mathews, whose architectural talents had greatly enhanced the relationship of the garden to the house, as well as to the surrounding vistas.

Over time, step by step, without any particular plan in the beginning, I added gardens and garden features on either side of the Tapis Vert, a long swath of lawn which constitutes the garden's main axis, until today the gardens cover about twenty acres and provide a diversity of horticultural experiences.

Terraces and steps planted with alpines lead down from the house to the Tapis Vert, and adjacent to

Below: *Densely planted beds line the perennial allée.*

Opposite: *The water course, bordered by an allée of thuya, gently runs down to a lake.*

it is a raised white garden centred on an oval pool filled with white water-lilies. A transverse axis starts in the white garden, crosses the Tapis Vert and a flanking rose garden underplanted with pinks, and extends through the main perennial allée. Another perennial allée, known as the Goose Allée, flanks the Tapis Vert to the north. From it thuya hedges and a rondel extend to a water course, a series of pools that gently cascade down the slope to Lac Libellule, a small lake to the west, created by damming a stream. The pools are filled with water-lilies and are framed with three varieties of decorative rhubarb.

Lac Libellule, named for the dragonflies that inhabit it, is surrounded by plantings that provide colour throughout the gardening season. The stream that feeds into it emerges from a steep hillside some distance to the north, and it has been used as the focus for a stream garden which winds its way through pools, under bridges and past follies on its course to the lake. Below the lake the stream winds through a deep ravine that stretches to a woodland pool where a Japanese pavilion is to be built. Two swinging rope bridges cross the

ravine, which is filled with large-leaved plants, mostly of Asiatic origin.

The trouble with gardening is that the hoped-for moment of perfection, if achieved, is fleeting at best, and in no time remedial work is needed to set things aright. There just do not seem to be any durable laurels for the weary horticulturalist to rest upon.

Above left: *A sea of naturalized narcissi underplant the trees in the orchard.*

Above right: *The stream garden features a series of bridges and many native plants dug from the surrounding countryside.*

Left: Iris sibirica, Iris pseudacorus *and naturalized lupins are mirrored in Lac Libellule.*

THE GARDEN OF

JOCELYNE TURCOTTE
POINTE AU PIC, QUÉBEC

Above: A bench flanked by Picea blanca.

Opposite: Beyond the formal garden, fields of wild flowers stretch down to the St Lawrence River.

It was a cold April day in 1980 when I first visited our property. Sitting on one hundred rolling acres overlooking the majestic St Lawrence River, the old house built in 1847 looked charming... and a bit mysterious.

As spring unfolded, however, the splendour of the scenery and the environment, the immensity of the vistas and the large grounds clearly took precedence over the house. The magnificent fields were covered with lupins and wild flowers. To the south, the river was their natural border and, on the east and west, tall Lombardy poplars seemed to be protecting them.

Closer to the house, large domestic gardens, contained within stone walls built by the townsfolk several years before, had been allowed to deteriorate.

My decision was taken. Our first challenge would be to give life and light again to the old gardens. Several years later, while not totally completed – a garden never is – the task is well under way.

The "grand jardin," with its large and colourful assortment of perennials and annuals, lies in the shadow of two huge poplar trees and of assorted fruit trees. There, *Lysimachia punctata*, Oriental poppies, irises, dianthus, impatiens and phlox all bring the garden back to life. The flowerbeds here are surrounded and protected by stone walls. Beyond, wild flowers and lupins grow limitlessly in the spring.

It is from the terrace, facing the south and west, that the view is most complete. Two *Picea blanca* on each side of an old bench

complete this place of rest from where one can admire the gardens, the fields, the tall mountains in the background and the river below.

On the side of the terrace protected from northern winds, my husband grows a variety of beautiful roses. They bloom all summer and into the fall, and provide a great spectacle from the dining-room windows. We also have a cutting garden, a vegetable garden and a raspberry patch that attracts visitors in late July.

I will never forget that first summer of 1980. Everything was in need of attention – the house, the garden, the fruit trees. But over the years, the designing and building of the gardens has been my project and my great joy.

Above far left: *A symmetrical planting of ornamental cabbages.*

Below far left: *A Quebec interpretation of a classical potager, its beds bordered by local stones.*

Above: *Yellow clusters of lysimachia and bearded iris dominate all four borders in summer.*

Below: *The main garden is enclosed by a quadrangle of perennial borders whose colours mirror each other.*

Opposite: A carefully planned vista is the dominant feature of this pleasure garden.

Right: *A massive planting of hostas.*

Below: *Plantings of red and white begonias add summer colour to the formal arrangement of clipped pyramidal yews.*

THE GARDEN OF

BERYL IVEY

LONDON, ONTARIO

Little evidence remained of the once resplendent pleasure garden that had flourished in the two-and-a-half-acre property my husband bought in 1960. For the next ten years, overgrown bushes and trees were removed or trimmed and the best of the perennials were set aside in nurseries for later replanting. The turning point was 1972: Duncan MacGregor became the resident gardener, and we enclosed an outer terrace at the back of the house to create a solarium. Most of the present gardens were designed from the vantage point offered by this room.

The long vista from the solarium overlooks the gently rising lawn that terminates in a

treed area at the back of the garden. Here tulip, walnut and beech trees of the south mingle with birch and pine trees of the north, metasequoia and ginkgo provide added interest and the filtered light beneath the canopy supports drifts of shade-tolerant day lilies and hostas.

The mature trees bordering the middle lawn serve as a background to a varied display of flowering shrubs and perennials.

From the old nurseries we reset peonies, Siberian and spuria iris, lysimachia, garden heliotrope and oenothera, and have introduced lythrums, delphiniums, veronica, scabiosa, achillea and others. Annuals give added colour where needed; some of my old favourites include nasturtiums, verbena, blue salvia, stocks and zinnias.

Duncan and I have learned by trial and error. In planting, we consider not only the colour but

the height and structure of each group as well as the size, shape and texture of the leaves. The colours of green throughout the garden are most important to me and so I use ground cover, particularly pachysandra, ivy and vinca under many of the tree groupings, and euonymus and pyracantha on walls.

I also keep a small wild-flower garden with ferns and Solomon's seals, trilliums, bluebells and

yellow lady slippers, and a small frog pond with marsh-marigolds, pulmonaria, polyanthus, red lobelia and, of course, frogs.

For me the garden is an oasis, a place of quiet beauty where birds, bees and butterflies mingle with rabbits and squirrels, and any people who might wish to find enjoyment here. Only cats are not welcome!

Below left: *Massed perennials and roses enclose an intimate garden room off the main vista.*

Below: *Informal plantings of perennials lead to the conservatory and potting shed.*

Bottom: *A classic ivy-covered wall is a backdrop for vibrant summer annuals.*

Opposite: The conditions of this seaside garden are identical to those of alpine and high-latitude regions.

Top left: Brilliant gentians bloom in front of Andromeda polyfolia.

Top right: Pink alpine azalea and Andromeda polyfolia.

Below left: The white bark of a birch tree is an effective foil for this collection of miniature specimen daffodils and rhododendrons.

Below right: Primulas grow out of a crack in a dry-stone wall by the house.

Over: Heathers, conifers, thymes, dwarf rhododendrons, other miniature specimens and native ericaceous plants nestle in skilfully arranged plantings.

THE GARDEN OF

WALTER OSTROM
INDIAN HARBOUR, NOVA SCOTIA

I ndian Harbour is a small fishing village located next to Peggy's Cove on Nova Scotia's south shore. It is a world dominated by granite and the sea. The cool, windy, foggy climate and shallow peaty soils between the boulders favour such wonderful native plants as rhodora *(Rhododendron canadense)*, bog laurel *(Kalmia polifolia)* and foxberry *(Vaccinium vitis-idaea)*. It took me a while to realize that the conditions of my seaside garden are, paradoxically, identical to high latitude and alpine regions. It explains the success I have had with dwarf rhododendrons, cassiopes and

Above: *Dwarf rhododendrons, creeping phlox and conifers complement each other.*

Right: *A* Picea nidiformis *surrounded by crowberry, woolly thyme and* Thymus serpyllum.

other ericaceous plants from the alpine regions of Japan, China and North America.

The cool moist summers here give way to brilliantly sunny, open winters. Although the lack of snow is tough on the plants, I find that I look at them more keenly during the winter when so much of the world is bare. I am interested in developing a winter garden and appreciate those plants that add interest with their texture, coloured foliage, bark or berries. Many natives such as wintergreen (*Gaultheria procumbens*), winterberry (*Ilex verticillata*) and lowbush blueberry (*Vaccinium angustifolium*) combine well with coloured forms of heathers, conifers and dwarf rhododendrons. I hope ultimately to provide good growing conditions for my plants and visual interest throughout the year.

Gardens may take generations to construct but the activity of gardening is a reward in itself. Propagating and planting are always full of promise; weeding is a task that brings an immediate sense of achievement. My garden, I have found, keeps me in touch with a world much larger than my own.

Above: Primula japonica *in the bog garden in spring.*

Above right: A close-up of a rudbeckia and coreopsis.

Below: Rudbeckia in the garden, a field of wild flowers beyond them.

Right: A raised cottage-style bed of daisies, larkspur, feverfew, hostas, candy tuft and other perennials.

THE GARDEN OF

JOHN MACKEEN

ST ANDREWS, NEW BRUNSWICK

This garden is of recent origin. Like the house it surrounds, it can be said to have travelled, most of the plants in it having once been part of a garden in the St John River Valley (roughly one hundred miles from here) where, until the autumn of 1982, the house stood. Now it overlooks Passamaquoddy Bay, an arm of the Bay of Fundy, and an inland garden has become a coastal one. Only the heathers had difficulty at first in adjusting to this exposed headland.

The garden is chiefly composed of perennials, mostly of the old-fashioned sort, grown in raised beds at either end of the house. Various wild flowers find a place

here too. The front of the house, with its southern exposure, is becoming the preserve of plants that relish long hours of sun and can cope with rather dry soil. Lavender, thyme and helianthemum are all doing well there and, as early as March, snowdrop, crocus and scilla.

The soil in these beds is largely sand. Compost and seaweed are worked into them every spring. The good drainage provided by raised beds is of real importance on land where a sandstone ledge is nowhere very far beneath the surface of the ground.

On the north side of the house, a garden of acid-loving plants is the latest venture. Here, with the shelter given by a low stone wall and, beyond it, a cedar hedge, the heathers are now doing well and so, too, are azaleas and various native wild plants, including laurels, crowberry, cranberry, blueberry and mayflower (trailing arbutus). Because many of these are evergreen, there is a measure of colour in the garden in all seasons.

Above: *A naturalistic planting of crown vetch, yellow daisies and phlox in front of the house.*

Opposite: *A low dry-stone wall flanks a massing of iris and yellow rudbeckia.*

Top above: *Climbing old-fashioned roses ramble over a wall of the house and an old stone well.*

Above: *Shell-pink Early Morn roses frame a window of the house.*

Right: *Foxgloves and annual geraniums are planted against and in a stone wall typical of the area.*

Top far right: *An American Pillar rose climbs a fence.*

THE GARDEN OF

JANET PIERS
CHESTER, NOVA SCOTIA

Gardening by the sea has its own joys – and challenges. I try to plant everything against a protective background, and as most of the garden faces south I have a fair amount of success. In a sunken wall garden I grow roses, azaleas and foxgloves – masses of them.

I also have a wonderful mixture of flowers and vegetables mixed in together. For instance, there is a bed of asparagus surrounded by masses of calendulas, the seeds of which I "stole" from a monastery garden – all the better for being stolen! Then, around my vegetable "chard yard," which grows beautifully on top of the compost heap, I have nasturtiums. The perennial beds, my "Friendship Garden," boast a Japanese peony that is nearly a hundred years old. I grow lettuce and parsley around one of the perennial beds, and there is always a patch of dill and some garlic and clusters of tomatoes wherever there's an empty spot.

Last year a special friend gave me English lavender and, thank goodness, it is flourishing. Behind the lavender are the hollyhocks, which are terribly important because each year they bring two beautiful humming-birds. Then there are three abundant grape vines that attract starlings. At the moment, inspired by a trip to Japan, I am trying to start a moss garden.

We do all the work ourselves, except for the grass cutting. One must always be fighting in a garden – fighting the slugs and earwigs that undermine our efforts. Sometimes we win, sometimes they do. It's all a challenge, but when it comes, victory is so sweet!

Left: *Sweet peas flank the garden fence at water's edge.*

Top: *A meandering path follows the sea wall.*

Above: *This climbing American Pillar rose is thought to have been brought to the property by its original settlers in 1759.*

THE GARDEN OF

MARGUERITE VAUGHAN
ST ANDREWS, NEW BRUNSWICK

Although my family has summered in St Andrews since I was a girl, we didn't buy this property until 1950. The house, a cottage designed by Canadian architect E.S. Maxwell and built in 1908, is set on several acres of land leading to Passamaquoddy Bay.

I had always wanted to create a garden with lots of roses, a garden roughly the size of a tennis court, but here we had much more ground. I needed help in planning, and in 1952 began to work closely with Laura McTavish, a Canadian-born landscape architect who was well known for her

work in the Boston area.

We laid out an enclosed garden behind the house where we planted roses, lilies, delphinium, phlox, a tree peony, begonias, carnations and many other species of blooming plants. We also added shrubs and vines such as euonymus, forsythia, dogwood,

Far left above: *A border of day lilies and nasturtiums in the cutting garden.*

Far left below: *Geraniums add a splash of colour to one of the walls of the house.*

Left: *A sea of day lilies and hostas surrounds a fountain near the house.*

Over: *A vast swath of fireweed in the distance provides a wonderful contrast to the cultivated garden.*

Above: *Raised beds of tuberous begonias and brightly coloured annuals border an enclosed garden by the house.*

Right: *An espaliered tree in the enclosed garden.*

Opposite above: *The cutting garden.*

Opposite below: *A sculpture by Lynn Chadwick, one of many that adorn this garden.*

climbing honeysuckle and clematis, as well as periwinkle for ground cover. An espaliered apple was planted against a fence to create a particular point of interest.

I much prefer perennials to annuals, but in my cutting garden I have planted snapdragons, zinnias, salvia and marigolds, in addition to roses and perennials, to provide colourful bouquets from early summer through fall.

The gardens are also a setting for the sculpture my late husband and I collected over the years—works by Lynn Chadwick and Sorel Etrog, among others.

We have tried to create a harmonious blend of the man-made and the natural in this magnificent setting, from sculpture and formal plantings to the drifts of wild flowers that stretch to the woods and beyond them to the bay.

I have been coming here for many years, but each summer is still filled with pleasure—both unexpected and familiar.

THE GARDEN OF

FREEMAN PATTERSON
SHAMPERS BLUFF, NEW BRUNSWICK

I had my first flower garden when I was about ten, my passion fuelled and my direction determined by my father, a farmer who was for vegetables and against flowers. I was for flowers and against my father – about the only visible expression of childhood rebellion I was ever permitted. My father did not make things easy for me, once digging up a rose bush in my absence because he feared "it might spread" and allowing an old sow to root around freely in my beds of nasturtiums, clarksia and asters. War was never actually declared, but it was fought nonetheless. At issue were the nature and value of beauty.

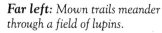

Far left: *Mown trails meander through a field of lupins.*

Left: *A carpet of bunchberries in bloom.*

Above: *One of the trails through the woods.*

Right: *An early frost outlines blueberry leaves.*

Opposite: *The cedar trail in winter.*

Today, just four kilometres from the scene of battle, I live surrounded by ever-changing fields and woods of wild and naturalized plants. It is their place as much as mine. In the traditional sense, I hardly garden at all. There are no beds of roses here, no formal plantings of any kind, just a couple of informal perennial borders. Instead, I mow paths and open spaces through the fields and old pastures to provide easy access to the continuing succession of wild plants – rock piles covered with sumac and hay-scented ferns, sweeps of bluets, stands of Canadian rhododendron, spirea, columbines, daisies and dozens of other flowering species. Among them I have scattered the seeds of Russell lupins that bloom by the thousands in June. In late summer and autumn, asters and goldenrods mix with silver and bronze grasses in richly textured carpets. In winter, stalks and seed heads, often hanging with snow or encased in ice, give pleasure.

In the forest I have carried out a program of selective cutting, removed debris and planted a few species of native trees that were missing. Nature has done the rest. There has been an explosion of plant species. Near the edge of the woods I have planted daffodils at random, and the bright yellow flowers accent stands of white birches in April and May. Like the lupins in the fields, the daffodils blend with the wild plants, yet serve as reminders that a human being lives here too and cares for this place.

About the Gardeners

PRINCESS NICHOLAS ABKHAZI, now eighty-six, is a talented pianist who divides her time between her garden, her dogs and her friends.

Now retired, CYRIL and MARY BAKER have travelled extensively and have even tried to garden in Saudi Arabia. They were among the founding members of the Rock Garden Society's Ontario Club, which now boasts hundreds of members.

SHIRLEY BEACH'S keen interest in gardening developed after her children were grown. She and her husband, now retired, are members of the Hardy Plant Group of the Victoria Horticultural Society.

ANGELA BOWERING is a college English teacher who has also published several works of literary criticism. Influenced by Gertrude Jeckyll's collaboration with Edwin Lutyens, her garden has won two British Columbia Nursery Trades awards.

FRANCIS CABOT is a horticultural enthusiast who devotes most of his time now that he is retired, to gardening. His special interests are growing alpines and woodland plants and designing and developing new gardens, each quite different from the next.

MARGARET CLARKE is a retired teacher who remains active as a volunteer worker at the local library and as a choir member and archivist at her church.

With twenty years of experience as a working member of the Auxiliary of the Royal Botanical Garden in Hamilton, Ontario, ELAINE CORBET is a member of the British Columbia Alpine Garden Club and also works on the University of British Columbia's Friends of the Garden Hotline.

AL CUMMINGS is a well-known Toronto-based packager of books for both Canadian and international publishers.

MARY DOVER has enjoyed careers in both the military, where she became a Lieutenant Colonel during the Second World War, and municipal politics in Calgary. Her loves are gardening, reading about gardens and all things Canadian, and travelling.

MARGUERITE VAUGHAN ELLER has lived in the United States and Mexico as well as Canada. A noted collector of art, she sits on the board of the International Council of the Museum of Modern Art in New York.

Born in Vancouver, a graduate of McGill University and the recipient of several honorary degrees, ARTHUR ERICKSON is one of Canada's most distinguished architects. His most recent large commission was for the new Canadian embassy in Washington.

BARBARA FRUM'S work as a broadcaster, journalist and author is known to virtually all Canadians. In addition to gardening, she and her husband collect Canadian paintings and tribal art from around the world.

BERYL IVEY has had a lifelong interest in wildlife and the environment. She has also been involved for many years as a volunteer in organizations that support the arts, most notably theatre, ballet and the visual arts.

EVELYN LAMBART is a graduate of the Ontario College of Art who worked at the National Film Board. She is now retired and gardening full-time.

A Master Gardener, RITA LEHMANN has worked with the Department of Agriculture in British Columbia. She now works with other volunteers answering questions on the Van Dusen Gardens' plant information hotline.

As a result of their interest in gardening, PATRICK LIMA and JOHN SCANLAN have now begun to earn their livings in the field. Patrick Lima is the author of two gardening books published by *Harrowsmith*. John Scanlan, a graduate of the Ontario College of Art, is a painter and has taken many of the photographs in Patrick's books.

JOHN MACKEEN teaches English at the University of New Brunswick in St John and also in Fredericton.

SUSAN MCCUTCHEON is active in many business and volunteer organizations. Her passions include reading and opera.

Born in England, VERONICA MILNER is a flower and landscape painter and Fellow of the Royal Society of Arts in London, England.

TOM and JOYCE MULOCK farm five hundred acres near Toronto, Ontario. Ardent travellers, they also collect English porcelain.

WALTER OSTROM is a potter and director of the Ceramics Department at the Nova Scotia College of Art and Design. Always interested in gardens, he specializes in making vases.

BILL and ANNE PETERS's gardening began with Bill's love of trees. They now operate a nursery business.

With her husband, Admiral Desmond Piers, JANET PIERS has travelled extensively. Now retired, she is very active in the community life of Chester, Nova Scotia.

THÉRÈSE ROMER DE BELLEFEUILLE took her law degree at Oxford University. She is a self-taught conference interpreter in English, French, Spanish and Polish.

JOSEPH SEGAL is a successful entrepreneur who has developed several businesses. He is very active in many community charities and has received the Golden Heart Community Achievement Award and the Vancouver Award for Entrepreneur of the Year.

REBECCA SIMARD is a businesswoman who is also an avid golfer and tennis player.

Dividing their time between Toronto and their property in Caledon, AMY and CLAIR STEWART have been enthusiastic gardeners for more than forty years.

When MARY TALBOT is not gardening, she is quilting, reading and collecting gardening books. Since there is no running water on her property, she collects the water she needs in rain barrels.

JACK TODD is an ardent conservationist who is active in several wildlife organizations concerned with protection of wildlife. For more than thirty years, one of his great pleasures has been teaching swimming to the blind.

When not in her garden or with her family, JOCELYNE TURCOTTE can be found sculpting in her studio. She is presently working on a stone bench for her garden.

MARGUERITE VAUGHAN has lived in the United States and Mexico as well as Canada. A noted collector of art, she sits on the board of the International Council of the Museum of Modern Art in New York.

INDEX

Figures in **bold type** indicate references in captions for photographs.

Book Design: V. John Lee
Production Director: Dianne Craig
Typography: Attic Typesetting Inc.
Graphic Assembly: Eleonore Richter, Universal Communications
Printer: New Interlitho Inc., Italy